NORTHERN COUNTIES BUSES DURING AND AFTER DEREGULATION

HOWARD WILDE

AMBERLEY

First published 2019

Amberley Publishing
The Hill, Stroud
Gloucestershire, GL5 4EP

www.amberley-books.com

Copyright © Howard Wilde, 2019

The right of Howard Wilde to be identified as
the Author of this work has been asserted in
accordance with the Copyrights, Designs and
Patents Act 1988.

ISBN 978 1 4456 9524 2 (print)
ISBN 978 1 4456 9525 9 (ebook)

British Library Cataloguing in Publication Data.
A catalogue record for this book is available from
the British Library.

Typesetting by Aura Technology and Software
Services, India. Printed in the UK.

Contents

Introduction

A brief history

Northern Counties Motor & Engineering Company Limited was established in Wigan, Lancashire, on 11 November 1919. The company commenced building vehicle bodywork, initially for new cars of the day. By 1921, single-deck bus and charabanc bodies were being produced, and, following the cessation of car production in 1923, this was to prove to be the way forward. The company then produced its first double-deck body on a Maudsley chassis in 1928.

As the decades passed, Northern Counties grew to become a major supplier to bus companies across the British bus industry. From the independent operators, to the small and large corporation fleets, to fleets of the British Electric Traction and Scottish Motor Traction groups, Northern Counties' coachwork could be found on a variety of different bus chassis throughout the land.

Probably the most notable association was with the SELNEC Passenger Transport Executive. SELNEC – an acronym for 'South East Lancashire North East Cheshire' – was created as a result of the Transport Act 1968, to assume control in November 1969 of twelve corporation fleets within the area, and was one of four similar PTE set-ups covering various metropolitan regions in England. Northern Counties was heavily involved with SELNEC from the outset, working to produce a specific double-deck body design, to help standardise a fleet that had a bewildering array of different designs inherited from the legacy corporation fleets. Twenty-one prototypes – six Leyland Atlanteans and fifteen Daimler Fleetlines – were bodied between 1971 and 1972, based on orders from the former municipal fleets of Ashton-under-Lyne, Bury and Rochdale. Production vehicles appeared the following year, again on Atlantean and Fleetline chassis, with bodywork by Northern Counties and, in the majority at first, Park Royal Vehicles of London.

In April 1974, SELNEC became Greater Manchester PTE, trading as Greater Manchester Transport following local government reorganisation that saw the establishment of Greater Manchester Council. As regards vehicle policy, it was business as usual for the new PTE, and the Standard as it became known, produced in the main now by NCME, was all pervading.

It could be said that the SELNEC/GMT Standard body ultimately defined Northern Counties and became its greatest legacy. 2,476 of the 2,836 Standards produced for both PTE fleets were bodied by Northern Counties; this figure included the prototypes and the ninety examples built for the associated Lancashire United Transport fleet after purchase by GMPTE in 1976. The same basic body style was also supplied to a variety of other operators, and also in amended format on different chassis supplied to both GMT and many other fleets. Northern Counties' status as GMPTE's preferred double-deck coachbuilder was fully cemented when the PTE purchased a 49 per cent share in Northern Counties in 1983.

However, things were about to change dramatically. The Transport Act 1985 brought about a major reform in the regulation of bus services. The official introduction of the legislation on 26 October 1986 ushered a new word into the industry vocabulary: deregulation. Gone were the rigid requirements for obtaining operator licences and registering bus services. Corporations and PTEs were required to separate their bus businesses into arms-length limited companies. The hitherto nationalised National Bus Company and Scottish Bus Group fleets were to be sold off to the private sector. The market was thrown wide open to near unfettered competition between companies new and established. The manufacturing sector, Northern Counties included, would feel the brunt of the uncertainty of those early deregulated days, as operators became extremely cautious over purchasing new buses in such uncertain times. There was eventually a gentle growth in confidence within a few years, however, and orders started to increase. Some of these were from the fledging companies formed under the new regime that were now themselves feeling a little more adventurous. Despite this, times were extremely challenging. The UK economy as a whole had dipped into recession in the middle of 1990 and, with the company over its overdraft limit and orders dried up, Northern Counties was placed into administration in May 1991.

Thankfully this setback was short-lived and the administrators managed to successfully restructure the business as a going concern. NCME continued trading and orders started to come in again. In October 1991 the company unveiled a new single-deck design, also rebranding its entire model range as 'Countybus'. Individual model names were allocated the following year; Palatine for double-deckers and Paladin for the new single-deck design.

In 1995 Northern Counties was purchased by Henlys Group plc, owner of established UK coachbuilder Plaxton. Both NCME and Plaxton were operated side by side at first, each with their own respective designs. A new single-deck low-floor body design, the Prestige, was introduced in 1996, initially manufactured at Wigan.

Rationalisation followed when Paladin and Prestige production was transferred to Plaxton's Scarborough plant and badged accordingly. Production of the Paladin came to an end in 1998, with the last few Prestige bodies delivered in 1999. Palatine production carried on at Wigan until 1999. The Wigan factory remained open to build Plaxton's new President low-floor double-deck body on Dennis Trident and Volvo B7TL chassis; but, even though bodies continued to be numbered in the same NCME series right until the end, the Northern Counties name was never used again.

August 2000 saw the announcement of a joint venture between Henlys and its rival, Mayflower Corporation, who were owners of UK firms Alexander and Dennis. The new entity was named TransBus International, and Dennis, Alexander and Plaxton came under its control, with TransBus-branded bodies produced at Wigan as a result.

Unfortunately the venture was not a success. Mayflower, the majority shareholder in the partnership, collapsed, forcing TransBus into administration in March 2004.

One of the companies to emerge from the TransBus failure was Alexander Dennis, who remain a major player in bus manufacturing to this day. Although they initially took on the Wigan plant, sadly there was to be no place for it in their new structure. On 26 January 2005, following completion of outstanding President orders, it closed for good, bringing to an end over eighty-five years of production in the town.

About this book

As the title suggests, this is a pictorial record of some of Northern Counties' output in its later years, set within the context of the deregulation era, together with a wider selection of the many older vehicles still putting in faithful service during those eventful years.

Some of the buses featured are as they were when newly into service; some are of images from later in life, owned by different operators, or painted in radically different liveries. There is also an occasional foray into London. Of course, deregulation never did come to the capital, despite it being an initial aspiration; however it turned out to be a lucrative market for Northern Counties nonetheless.

All photographs are my own, as are any opinions expressed. There have been numerous useful points of reference, to help glean particular data and to confirm event timelines, including various 'G-list' publications of the PSV Circle; the *Bus Handbook* fleet lists for north-west England, published by Capital Transport; the erstwhile *Fleetbook* series of A. M. Witton, indispensable among all young enthusiasts in the seventies and eighties; the Wikipedia website, including links to specific extracts from *Commercial Motor*; Alan Millar's article about TransBus, 'Two Davids, Three Johns and Two Brians', within *Buses Yearbook 2006*, edited by Stewart J. Brown, published by Ian Allan; the late Revd Eric Ogden's *Northern Counties of Wigan*, published by Transport Publishing Company in 1976; and Alan Millar's *ABC Bus & Coach Recognition Fifth Edition* from 2007, published by Ian Allan. Particularly useful has been the excellent Bus Lists on the Web website, which provided vital information regarding vehicle identities, chassis and body numbers, dates and so on.

This book is not intended to be a definitive history of either Northern Counties or deregulation itself. Instead, it is a series of snapshots to capture the colour and variety of this fascinating period, and to pay tribute to a much-loved and much-missed builder of buses in what, at the time of writing, would have been its centenary year.

I very much hope that you enjoy.

Howard Wilde
May 2019

Chapter One
Deregulation

Whether or not deregulation was a good thing is a debate for elsewhere. One thing that can be said though is that it caused great upheaval within the bus industry at the time. Northern Counties found that year-on-year orders from its regular customers could no longer be taken as guaranteed and that diversification and resilience were required. The industry at the time veered heavily towards the concept of high-frequency van-derived minibus operation. NCME joined a number of builders offering such a product, in its case on Dodge (later Renault) or Iveco chassis, which provided considerable output for the business for a time. The minibus revolution was relatively short-lived however and, although there still remained a considerable niche market for such vehicles, confidence in full-sized buses gradually returned as the years progressed.

Early deregulation saw GM Buses diversify seriously into minibus operation. 360 vehicles were purchased in just over twelve months, 230 of which were from Northern Counties on Dodge (later Renault) S56 chassis. One of the first, 1811, actually arrived into GMT ownership before deregulation in July 1986 and is captured here in Ashton-under-Lyne in 1988, demonstrating the Little Gem identity that was eventually adopted.

Of course, the reason for GM's sudden fondness for the minibus was the arrival of Bee Line Buzz Company, owned then by United Transport International. This was one of fifty Dodge S46s taken into stock between 1986 and 1987, but photographed some years later with a much-changed Bee Line, on Lever Street in Manchester, December 1994.

Another Dodge S46, very similar to the Bee Line vehicles, was this example in service with Bolton Coachways, in Blackburn in June 1989. By several twists and turns it ended up with GM Buses North in 1995.

Warrington 102 was one of six Dodge S56s bought in 1987, and painted in a dedicated blue and yellow livery. It is pictured in April 1990 in the rather depressing bus station of the time, since redeveloped into a much-improved interchange.

Looking creditably smart for an eight-year-old van-derived minibus is this Iveco with JP Travel of Middleton pictured in central Manchester in 1995. It was new in 1987 as a Northern Counties demonstrator and was exhibited at the Commercial Motor Show of that year, painted in GM Buses Little Gem colours. However GM only ever had it on loan briefly, before it went off on demonstration to other operators.

Merseybus purchased twenty-seven new NCME-bodied Dodge/Renault S56s between 1986 and 1988. What was their 7668 still carries their maroon and cream livery in this shot from June 1993, but now under the ownership of Pennine Blue and pictured 40 miles due east in Ashton-under-Lyne.

In 1987 Northern Counties introduced a revised minibus body for the Renault S56, with a more stylised appearance. Independent operator Heaton of Leigh took delivery of two of these during 1988. The town's bus station is the location in November 1992.

Municipal Preston faced a deregulation scrap with the second of the United Transport minibus operations, Zippy, and amassed forty-seven Renault S56s between 1987 and 1988. Number 78, being the later style, is pictured in the bus station in April 1991.

Northern Counties bodied eight Renault S75 minibuses for GM Buses to operate Greater Manchester PTE-supported accessible services that mirrored regular commercial routes, a far cry from today's nigh-on universal low-floor bus operation. The first, 1721, is pictured at rest in Stockport bus station in May 1991.

In 1988 Northern Counties entered into a deal with French manufacturer Renault to produce a body on its well-established PR100 single-deck chassis. The venture unfortunately was not a success and only five examples were built: a solitary vehicle for London Buses, three buses for Luton Airport and this, the first of the five, which was a demonstrator. A cold morning in November 1990 sees it arrive into Manchester, on hire to Blackburn Transport, at the end of the long run on service 702.

Delivered to Nottingham City Transport, between October 1986 and January 1987, was a trio of rare Leyland Lion underfloor-engined buses, with NCME bodywork to Nottingham's individualistic styling. Number 392 is pictured in the city centre in October 1997.

This GM Buses MCW Metrobus was one of thirty that were unique in having bodywork by Northern Counties. Initial examples, such as 5206, were actually new to GMPTE just before deregulation, with delivery continuing into the ownership of the new company. 5206 was more unusual still, being one of ten out of the thirty powered by Cummins rather than Gardner engines. The Metrobuses, along with corresponding Leyland Olympians of the time, featured this Express livery and coach seats for use on limited stop services. Manchester Piccadilly bus station in October 1990 is the location.

The order for GM's final twenty-eight Leyland Olympians was cancelled at deregulation due to market uncertainty. They were eventually leased to London Buses in late 1987 as dealer stock vehicles for their Bexleybus operation. All later found their way onto an eager second-hand market and twenty-one were acquired by Tyne and Wear PTE's successor company, Busways, in 1991. Number 687 is seen on Grainger Street in Newcastle in May 1993.

In the end GM Buses did order replacement Olympians for the twenty-eight cancelled buses. Their arrival ushered in both a new livery for GM and body style revisions from Northern Counties, with a peaked dome and new-look front grille. 3284 stands in Piccadilly bus station in October 1988, when a month old, carrying an in-house side advert.

One of five Volvo B10Ms purchased by Derby (then council-owned) in 1988. Number 152 carries the later Blue Bus identity while waiting over near the bus station in this shot in 1993.

Yorkshire independent South Yorkshire Road Transport of Pontefract had been an occasional Northern Counties customer over the years. In 1988 they took this Leyland Olympian, registered with cherished mark TWY 7 from new. The number had previously been on a 1957 Leyland PD2 of theirs. The Olympian was eventually exported to Cyprus as an open-top sightseeing bus. The registration ended up being carried by several newer buses in the Arriva fleet.

A visitor from out of town: Chester's number 10 pictured in central Manchester in March 1994. This was the second of a pair of 10-metre low-height Olympians with coach seats supplied to them in April 1989.

Twelve Leyland Olympians, with bodywork by Northern Counties, were delivered to Cambus between late 1988 and early 1989. This example was in the subsidiary fleet of Viscount Bus and Coach and was photographed leaving Peterborough bus station in August 1994.

Yorkshire Rider, the deregulation successor to West Yorkshire PTE, bought Leyland Olympians with the peaked-dome body in both low- and full-height configurations. Low-height 5156 was photographed in Halifax in May 1994, carrying a commemorative livery for the erstwhile Todmorden UDC fleet.

An inter-group transfer by Stagecoach saw this Volvo B10M Citybus, one of a batch of twelve new in 1989, transferred from its original Southdown all the way north to Fife Scottish. The location for what became Fife 940 is Edinburgh's St Andrew Square bus station in August 1994.

Merseybus purchased forty Leyland Olympians in 1989, with the body order split fifty-fifty between Northern Counties and Alexander. NCME-bodied 259 wears the attractive maroon and cream livery of the time, pictured in central Manchester in April 1994. The bus was based at St Helens garage, branded up as Lancashire Travel, in direct competition with GM Buses North.

Fareway was formed at deregulation by former Merseyside drivers. Initially a substantial fleet of second-hand buses was built up competing against their former employer. Then, in 1989, the boat was pushed out and five impressive new long-wheelbase Leyland Olympians were acquired. Number 166 is captured approaching Lime Street in central Liverpool in May 1990.

Another Liverpool independent was Liverline, who purchased five new Scania N113 in early 1990. G34 HKY is seen in May that year. In the background, the Royal Court Theatre is advertising a variety of different acts, including James, former Blondie lead singer Deborah (originally Debbie) Harry and a dance music artist of the time called Guru Josh.

This was one of thirteen Leyland Olympians new to Kentish Bus in 1989. By October 1993 it was in service with British Bus subsidiary Midland Fox as their 4530, photographed in Leicester.

A change of ownership for Bee Line in 1989 saw them come under the control of Drawlane Group, with a move towards more conventional bus operation. Welcome additions to the fleet, to improve a rather dubious age profile, were four Volvo B10Ms, cascaded in from sister company London and Country in 1991 when only two years old.

Kentish Bus 550 was one of a large batch of Leyland Olympians delivered to them for London Transport-contracted services in 1990 and is parked up behind Centrepoint near Charing Cross Road in October 1995. The area nowadays has been completely transformed by Crossrail construction work.

London operator Pan Atlas received nine Leyland Olympian/Northern Counties in October 1989 for London Transport tendered work. This shot shows one of these, following a move north after acquisition by United, in Beverley in September 1995.

This was one of a batch of twenty-seven Volvo B10M Citybuses delivered to London Buses between 1989 and 1990 and photographed with London General, leaving Aldwych in October 1995.

Whippet of Fenstanton bought this Volvo B10M Citybus in September 1989, captured on a sunny day in Cambridge nineteen years later.

Long-established Manchester operator Mayne of Clayton invested in new Scania N113, taking five between 1989 and 1990. Number 17 was the last of the five and is pictured heading out into open countryside at Daisy Nook, between Ashton-under-Lyne and Droylsden, in September 1995.

Blazefield Holdings chose Northern Counties for bodywork on six Leyland Olympians for its Keighley and District subsidiary, delivered in August 1989. Here 336 is pictured entering the central bus station in Leeds in May 1994.

A sunny South Shields is the scene for this October 1995 view of Busways 675, one of a batch of ten Leyland Olympians. Most were based at Sunderland in the yellow and green variant of Busways' attractive livery, but this example sported the red and cream of their Economic unit.

Five NCME-bodied Scania N113 double-deckers were added to the Yorkshire Rider fleet in October 1990. Number 8008 passes through the lights at Eastgate in central Leeds four years later.

Preston's four NCME-bodied Leyland Olympians, purchased in 1991, had long lives, clocking up over a quarter of a century's service with the same operator. Number 104 was captured at work in 2005.

October 1995 saw major London Underground engineering work on the Northern Line, and numerous different buses were involved on rail replacement work. Here we see Capital Citybus 258, a Dennis Dominator/NCME, new to Front Runner South East in 1991, at Euston station.

East Kent 7806 was one of a batch of ten NCME-bodied Leyland Olympians for this operator, new between July and August 1990. The occasion is the Showbus rally in September 1991, held at Woburn Abbey. 7806 is marked up to commemorate East Kent's then diamond jubilee.

A trio of Leyland Olympians in the East Yorkshire fleet, captured in August 1992 on the open-parking ground adjacent to Hull Station. Note that East Yorkshire specified fixed rather than peaked domes.

GM Buses took delivery of twenty-five Northern Counties-bodied double-deckers between 1991 and 1992. The order comprised ten Dennis Dominators, five Scania N113s and ten Volvo B10M Citybuses. Pictured here are Dominator 2033, allocated to Princess Road; Scania 1465, working out of Hyde Road; and Bury-allocated B10M 7005. 7005 is pictured among Metrolink construction work on High Street in central Manchester, working a rail replacement service during the time the Bury line was being converted to Metrolink tram operation.

Chapter Two
Paladin and Prestige

Northern Counties unveiled the first single-decker from its new Countybus range – a Volvo B10M for GM Buses – at the Bus and Coach Show in October 1991. It initially intended to name the model Palatine, but by the following March the name Paladin was adopted instead, with the Palatine name applied solely to double-deckers. The Paladin proved to be a versatile and distinctive design, being built on numerous different chassis, in several different configurations and in various different styles.

The Prestige low-floor single-decker was introduced in 1996, following Northern Counties' takeover by Henlys the previous year, and was offered on Volvo B10BLE and DAF SB220 chassis. Production of both Paladin and Prestige eventually moved to Plaxton in Scarborough.

The inaugural body for what was to become the Paladin was built on a Volvo B10M chassis and entered service with GM Buses in November 1991. It is pictured on service in central Manchester the following April, still carrying the allocation sticker from its native Wigan garage to where it would subsequently return.

South Yorkshire Transport took a solitary Paladin-bodied Dennis Dart, painted in its colourful Mainline livery. It is pictured when brand new at a bus rally at the Meadowhall shopping centre in September 1992.

Warrington Borough Transport purchased Dennis Darts with Paladin bodies. Their number 221 is pictured in the town centre in April 1993, carrying the distinctive blue and yellow Midi Lines livery of the time.

Huyton-based independent Liverbus took eight Paladins on Volvo B10B chassis in 1993. Number 105 is pictured, looking very smart and displaying a full set of badges, in central Liverpool in August of that year.

London Buses purchased thirteen Volvo B10Bs with Paladin double-door bodies in June 1993. VN10 is pictured passing through Trafalgar Square, branded up as Clapham Omnibus, in October 1994.

Just before the Volvo B10Bs were delivered to London, a batch of thirty-one Paladins on Dennis Lance chassis arrived in the capital between March and April 1993. What had been London Buses LN3 is seen much later in life with Diamond Bus in Birmingham in October 2006.

This Volvo B10B with a Paladin body had been new as a Volvo demonstrator in August 1993. By 2005 it had been bought by Stott of Oldham, and was photographed some way from home on a schools service in Hyde, in September that year.

A Paladin body on a very late Dennis Falcon chassis – in fact numerically the very last Falcon of all – with Leicester Citybus, photographed in the city centre in October 1993.

This Volvo B10B/Paladin was new to Scottish operator Whitelaw of Stonehouse in August 1993. Cambridge, fifteen years later in September 2008, is the scene with the bus owned by Go Whippet.

Fylde had four used Leyland Atlantean double-deck chassis rebodied with Paladin bodies in 1993. They had been part of the same batch, new originally with Alexander bodywork to Bradford Corporation in 1971. All retained their original registrations, as demonstrated by number 5 on Talbot Road in Blackpool in June 1994.

The Wellglade Group turned to Northern Counties to supply twenty-eight Volvo B10Bs with Paladin bodywork, delivered to their Trent and Barton fleets between August 1993 and January 1994. Nottingham is the location for Trent 120 in January 1995.

This was one of a trio of Paladin-bodied Dennis Darts for Arrowline (Star Line) of Knutsford, pictured at Altrincham Interchange in April 1995. The windscreen design didn't really suit this smaller chassis and the employment elsewhere by NCME of a revised 'wrap-round' design was a considerable improvement.

Kentish Bus 115 was one of a large batch of forty-five short (9-metre) Dennis Darts, new in 1994. The smaller middle side window emphasises the shorter length, as 115 passes by the Tower of London in the following October.

East Yorkshire 261, a lone Paladin-bodied Volvo B6 new in 1994, is pictured in Hull city centre in April 1996.

Mayne of Clayton took a pair of Scania L113s with Paladin bodies in November 1994. Number 42 is shown when brand new in central Manchester. The second example had been a second-hand Scania demonstrator, new a few months earlier.

Stagecoach had purchased Cleveland Transit by the time of this visit to Middlesbrough, in August 1995, and standard group vehicles, such as this Volvo B10M with a Paladin body, had recently entered service. There was, as can be seen, an initial agreement to retain Cleveland Transit colours as part of the takeover arrangement.

No such niceties at nearby Hartlepool, where an identical Volvo B10M from the same registered batch was captured in the town in full Stagecoach corporate livery on the same day.

Unusual variants from the norm for Stagecoach were five Volvo B10Ms with Paladin bodies that had been constructed to export specification for Stagecoach's Malawi operation, but instead ended up in Britain with South Coast Buses. They featured front- instead of side-mounted radiators, larger wheels and bonded glazing. In 2006 they were all transferred to Stagecoach Manchester, and 20605, originally new as L605 DCD, is pictured on Market Street in Hyde in April that year.

The first new vehicle purchases for GM Buses North were Volvo B6 single-deckers with Paladin bodies, featuring the wrap-round windscreen design. Number 1059 is depicted on service 135 on Corporation Street, Manchester, when new in October 1994. Its reduced-fare offers bear witness to the intense competition going on at the time.

After the Volvo B6 came Dennis Darts, again to the Paladin design, but this time without the distinctive stepped window line. GM Buses North 0617 is pictured leaving Town Square bus station in Oldham in August 1995.

Yorkshire Terrier was one of many independents to spring up in Sheffield at deregulation. Initially a prolific user of used Leyland Nationals (among other things), by November 1995 they had invested in new vehicles in the shape of six Paladin-bodied Dennis Darts. Number 109 is seen in the city centre when new that month.

Yorkshire Traction took a trio of Paladin-bodied Dennis Darts in late 1995. Number 430 was photographed on a grimy winter's day on Westgate in Huddersfield the following January.

Pictured waiting over in Leeds Central bus station in April 1996 is Yorkshire Traction 292, one of five Scania L113/Paladins new to them in September 1994.

C & M Travel of Aintree, hitherto an operator in the main of Leyland Nationals, purchased seven new Dennis Darts with Paladin bodies in October 1995. Number 2011 is seen in Derby Square in central Liverpool in January 1996.

A picturesque setting, as Pennine of Skipton's D7, a Paladin-bodied Dennis Dart, passes over the River Ribble from Settle into Giggleswick in June 2010. The driver has already set the blinds for the return journey to Skipton.

A smart Scania L113/Paladin pictured in Harrogate in June 2010, operated by Harrogate Coach Travel. The bus was new to Busways in September 1994, several months after Stagecoach purchased the company.

Leeds in February 1997, and this Paladin-bodied DAF SB220 is in service in all-over white with Geldard (Bigfoot Bus). The M-RCP registration denotes that the bus is another one of many from the Hughes-DAF dealership, new in February 1995 and operated initially by Speedlink.

After First Bus acquired GM Buses North in 1996, they added new vehicles to the existing fleet. Typical of these was this Paladin-bodied Dennis Dart, very similar to examples already in service, pictured heading out of Greengate arches in Salford when new in May of that year.

A brand-new Paladin on Scania L113 chassis for Bee Line, photographed on driver familiarisation duties in Newton Street, Manchester, in May 1997. The fleet was by then under the management of associate company North Western, as indicated by the fleet names carried on the colourful blue, red and yellow livery. Both companies were by this point owned by the Cowie Group, who would become Arriva that November.

A Paladin-bodied DAF SB220 in service with Manchester independent UK North of Gorton on Portland Street in Manchester in November 2005. The bus had first been operated by Speedlink in September 1996.

The first examples of Northern Counties' Prestige body were on five Volvo B10BLE low-floor chassis for Stagecoach Manchester. Their stay in Manchester turned out to be relatively brief and they were moved eventually to Stagecoach's Busways fleet in Newcastle, after seeing interim use in Cambridge. 604 is pictured near Mayne's garage on Ashton New Road in Clayton in April 1997.

This Prestige is not, as the badge would imply, a Plaxton, but in fact a Northern Counties example. It's also an unusual one, being a gas-powered DAF SB220 low-floor for First's PMT (Crosville) fleet. SAD882 turns from Frodsham Street into Foregate Street in the historic centre of Chester in September 1999.

Six Prestige bodies on DAF SB220 were taken by Go Ahead for their Gateshead and District fleet between April and May 1997. What became Go Northern 4823 is pictured in October 2005, approaching Gateshead Metro.

UK North acquired two DAF SB220/Prestiges, which had both originally been new to West Midlands Travel's Smiths subsidiary, the former Your Bus fleet, in September 1997. Number 110 was captured in Chorlton Street in Manchester in January 2005.

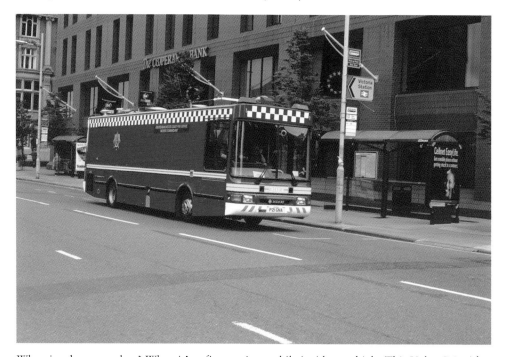

When is a bus not a bus? When it's a fire service mobile incident vehicle. This Volvo B6 with a Paladin body was purchased by Greater Manchester Fire Service in August 1996 and converted to its bespoke layout by specialist firm Saxon.

Chapter Three
Palatine

Initial Palatines from introduction in 1992 were very much to the existing double-deck design, but a revised model was introduced the following year. This featured bolder styling than before, with curved front upper-deck window and windscreen, and a revised front dash panel, in common with the Paladin. A simpler variant was also offered, more in keeping with the original design, which became known as the Palatine I; the more radical version was branded Palatine II. Like the related single-deck Paladin, the Palatine became a common sight in all variants in bus fleets across Britain, built on a number of different chassis. Production finally came to an end at the end of the decade, with the last examples entering service during 1999.

Stagecoach inherited a batch of 1992 London Buses Scania N113/Palatine when they bought into London, and then cascaded them elsewhere within the group when their working life in the capital was done. A number ended their days in Manchester, some in fleet colours and others in the Magic Bus fleet. Stagecoach Manchester 15343 is pictured in Portland Street, Manchester, on a January evening in 2009.

Blazefield Holdings purchased six Palatines on long-wheelbase Leyland Olympian chassis for their Yorkshire Coastliner operation. All six featured personal registration plates. Number 402, smartly painted in blue and cream, loads up at Leeds Central bus station, bound for Scarborough, in 1993.

Bristol Omnibus took delivery of thirty Leyland Olympians with Palatine bodies in January 1993. The subsequent merger of owners Badgerline and Grampian that formed First in 1995 eventually led to dispersal of the batch around the country, the first five being transferred north to PMT for the First Pennine operation. Further reorganisation saw this transferred into First Manchester control. 3312 is shown in their orange livery, around half a mile from Hyde town centre, in August 2001.

A wintery day in Chesterfield, November 1994, sees East Midland long-wheelbase Leyland Olympian/NCME Palatine 104 in full Stagecoach corporate livery, heading for Sheffield and the giant shopping centre at Meadowhall.

Another customer for long-wheelbase Olympians was famous independent OK Travel of Bishop Auckland, who had three for services into Newcastle. K108 YVN is pictured loading for Newcastle at Bishop Auckland in April 1995, its already handsome features enhanced further by OK's attractive red and cream livery.

This was numerically the last of four Volvo Olympian/Palatines, featuring coach seating, new to Western National in July 1993. By the time of this shot in Torquay in 1999, Western National was under First Group ownership and standard First branding had been added to the existing blue and white livery, but with the remains of the previous names still visible.

East Yorkshire added to existing numbers of Leyland Olympian/Northern Counties by purchasing a batch of twelve with Palatine bodies in 1993. 575 is captured looking commendably smart fifteen years later in Hull in October 2008.

First Manchester 30228, pictured in Manchester in October 2006, has the distinction of being the first Palatine II and the only example to be bodied on a Leyland Olympian chassis. It was chronologically the last of a batch of eight, new to Capital Citybus in April 1993, five months after its other conventional Palatine colleagues. All carried triple-eight registration marks, an indication of Capital Citybus's Hong Kong ownership, the number eight being a Chinese symbol of good fortune. The bus is now preserved.

A shot of an early Volvo Olympian with a Palatine II body for Liverbus, new in October 1993. This view in central Liverpool in March 1995 sees it carrying the name *Andy*, in memory of Liverbus employee Andy Wade, a mark that it subsequently carried throughout its working life and on into preservation.

Summer holiday time in Woolacombe, Devon, in June 2001, and First Red Bus 1817 has arrived in the small bus station working the service to nearby Ilfracombe. The Volvo Olympian/NCME Palatine was the last of a batch of three new to Red Bus's previous owner, North Devon, in November 1993.

Twenty-five Palatine I-bodied Volvo Olympians of both low- and normal-height configuration entered service with Yorkshire Rider in the summer of 1994, following the purchase of the company by Badgerline Holdings from its employees earlier that year. The Headrow in Leeds is the location for this shot of full-height 5401 the following October.

For a while in the nineties Cleveland Transit owned Hull City Transport. When Stagecoach acquired Transit, the Hull operation also formed part of the deal. As had been agreed in the North East, Stagecoach retained the existing livery for a while. As a result this 1995 Volvo Olympian/Palatine I carried the attractive blue, yellow and white Hull variant of the Transit livery in this view from April 1996.

Blackpool added six Volvo Olympian/NCME Palatine IIs to its fleet in November 1994. Number 378 is seen loading passengers in the town centre in August 1994.

Cowie purchased several Scania N113s with Palatine bodies for their Grey-Green operations on tendered London Transport routes. The attractive livery is demonstrated by 179, passing by the National Gallery to the north of Trafalgar Square in October 1995.

Manchester operator Wall's, having already taken modern single-deckers into stock, went for new double-deckers as well in the shape of five DAF DB250s with Palatine II bodies, delivered during 1995. All had personalised numbers on either M or N plates, including M20 WAL, pictured on Portland Street in Manchester in August that year.

Blue Bus of Horwich purchased two DAF DB250 with Palatine II bodies that originated with the Hughes-DAF dealership. Their 47, the second of the pair, had latterly seen service with Capital Citybus. The scene is Wigan bus station in July 1999.

Stagecoach purchased Palatine I-bodied Volvo Olympians for their London operations, including this example for Selkent, photographed on Regent Street in October 1995, when two months old.

Captured when brand new on its first day in service, on 1 February 1996, is Finglands 1745.
This was one of five Volvo Olympians with Palatine I bodies purchased for this EYMS Group
company. Manchester's Piccadilly bus station is the location.

Very smart additions to the Merseyside Transport fleet in 1996 were thirty-six long-wheelbase
Olympian/Palatine IIs. Number 0273 is captured in Whitechapel in Liverpool in February that
year, branded as Silver Service for services between Liverpool and Wirral via the Mersey tunnels.

Six new Volvo Olympian/NCME Palatine IIs were added to the East Yorkshire fleet in 1995. An impressive 587 of this batch was photographed parked up near Hull station in April 1996.

This was one of a trio of Palatine I-bodied Volvo Olympians, new to Selby and District – at that time a British Bus subsidiary – in May 1996. The bus was captured leaving Leeds bound for Micklefield the following February, by which time the company was owned by Cowie Group.

Leaside Bus Company, owned by Cowie, took delivery of nine DAF DB250/Palatine IIs in October 1995 for London operations. By the time of this shot in central Manchester in September 2006, this example had been transferred north to the Arriva North West fleet.

Transdev Lancashire United is the operator of this 1995 Volvo Olympian/NCME Palatine I, originally new to London Central. The bus had come into Transdev ownership after their takeover of Blackburn Transport, whose livery it still carries in this October 2007 shot in the town. Ironically, when new, the batch had been registered locally by Northern Counties with former Blackburn 'BV' marks.

Looking extremely smart is this ex-London Central Volvo Olympian/Palatine I in the fleet of Finch of Higher Ince, near Wigan. The location is the end of Boyle Street in Cheetham, Manchester, where the bus was taking part in a London-themed running day organised by the nearby Museum of Transport in 2009.

Bullock of Cheadle took four new dealer-stock Volvo Olympian/Palatine Is in September 1996 and operated them for a while in all-over white. This is demonstrated by P483 HBA, captured on Oxford Street in Manchester when recently delivered.

One of many similar double-deckers that Stagecoach specified throughout its empire, in this case with Viscount. 569 is a long-wheelbase Volvo Olympian with a Palatine I body, pictured in Peterborough in August 1997.

A Volvo Olympian with a Palatine II body in Northumbria's unusual red, white and grey livery, new to them along with ten others, in May 1997. Newcastle's Eldon Square bus station is the location in this view from October that year.

This Volvo Olympian with Palatine I body was new to London General in 1997. It still looked very much the London bus when photographed in Birmingham in October 2006, following an inter-group transfer by parent Go Ahead to their Diamond Bus operation.

The colourful livery of City Rider, the identity adopted for the Derby fleet by owners British Bus, is carried by this Volvo Olympian/Palatine I. The bus was one of three new in September 1996 and is pictured in the city the following August.

Seven Volvo Olympian/Palatine Is were delivered to Arriva Cymru in April 1998 to upgrade the mainline service between Chester and Wrexham, rebranded as Route One. DVV234 loads passengers on the Wales side, in Wrexham bus station, in September 1999.

Relatively rare in the UK bus market was the Dennis Arrow, the double-deck version of the Lance single-decker, with only seventy-three buses built. Northern Counties bodied twenty-two of these, including this example, new to Capital Citybus in 1996, and photographed in the First Manchester fleet in June 2007.

An inter-group transfer by Go-Ahead Group led to this Palatine I-bodied Volvo Olympian and several others finding a new home with Go North East. It had started life with their London Central fleet in 1998. Newcastle's famous Tyne Bridge, heading into Gateshead, is the location in August 2007.

A sunny day in Blackburn in May 2014 sees Transdev Lancashire United 984, a Volvo Olympian/ Palatine I carrying yellow school bus colours, filling in on local service work. The bus had been new to London Sovereign in 1998.

Rossendale 21 was a Volvo Olympian/Palatine I that was new to Metrobus in August 1998. It is pictured on schools work in Uppermill in May 2014, still carrying the livery of its previous owner.

In terms of the NCME body number series, the final Palatines were four Volvo Olympian/Palatine IIs, delivered to Bullock of Cheadle in January 1999. However there was a good number of earlier numbered Palatines still to enter service later into that year. Bullock's S959 URJ is pictured in Manchester's Piccadilly bus station when new.

Chapter Four
Buses Built Before Deregulation

In addition to the new buses produced, there was also a large number of earlier Northern Counties-bodied vehicles still in existence and in regular use. While the market for new builds was initially in the doldrums, the second-hand market conversely went through the roof, as operators old and new sourced a more 'pre-enjoyed' product in those uncertain and cost-conscious times. The used market for NCME-built buses was particularly buoyed by Greater Manchester PTE disposing of several hundred surplus vehicles at deregulation via dealer Kirkby Central. There were other used NCME-bodied examples being sold off and snapped up all over the industry, of course. The following is a small selection of those, either in passenger-carrying service, or fulfilling a non-PSV role of some kind. There is also a small selection of buses rescued by the preservationist movement and lovingly restored to their former glory, showcasing the Northern Counties of days gone by.

An August 1994 view in central Manchester of what was by then GM Buses North 4718, a fairly late Standard class Leyland Atlantean. Body construction was of aluminium alloy, replacing the previously used steel, featuring a one-piece staircase and rubber gasket windows, leading to the distinguished split front-upper-deck window arrangement.

A former GM Standard Leyland Fleetline from 1977, originally new to the subsidiary Lancashire United Transport fleet, in service with Fareway of Kirkby. This was one of a large number of Standards, among other types, that Fareway acquired when they set up competitive operations. A later livery is carried in this view in Liverpool city centre in April 1991.

Fellow Merseyside operator Liverbus of Huyton was also a keen advocate of the GM Standard, but in its case Atlanteans rather than Fleetlines were favoured. Their number 28, ex-GMT 7694, is seen in Liverpool, also in April 1991.

Stott of Oldham bought a considerable number of former GM Standards, initially Daimler Fleetlines and later some Leyland Atlanteans, mostly Northern Counties-bodied. YNA 300M is captured in the town centre in June 1994, wearing the company's attractive livery.

October 1995 in central Newcastle and this former GMT Standard Leyland Atlantean/Northern Counties in Annfield Plain is pictured loading up for Chester-le-Street.

Finglands of Rusholme 934 was one of many former GM Standards, both Atlantean and Fleetline, operated over the years. The location is Cross Street, opposite the Royal Exchange, in Manchester on New Year's Eve 1993, with passengers boarding for West Didsbury via the highly competitive Wilmslow Road.

Mayne of Clayton amassed a number of former GM Standards from the late eighties onwards. Two different types are captured together in Piccadilly, Manchester, in April 1997. On the right is a steel-framed Leyland Fleetline; while on the left is a later alloy-framed Leyland Atlantean, one of six purchased that proved to be Mayne's first and only Atlanteans.

A former GM Standard Leyland Fleetline in the Chesterfield fleet in November 1994. The Lancashire registration number reveals it to be one of the examples supplied to Lancashire United Transport while owned by GMPTE.

At deregulation, Yorkshire Rider made the decision not to take on the lease commitments of a significant number of Leyland Olympians from its predecessor, West Yorkshire PTE, and instead purchased second-hand ex-GM Standard Atlanteans and Fleetlines. Former GMT Atlantean 7765, now Yorkshire Rider 6417, is pictured on The Headrow in central Leeds in April 1993, alongside a branch of the now long-departed electrical retailer Rumbelows.

A remarkable rebuild that has the hallmarks of an apprentice training exercise. North Western 584, an ex-GM Standard Atlantean, had been involved in a collision with a dustbin lorry and was given this spectacular makeover as a result. A Leyland National front end and windscreen were grafted into place, while an NBC-style destination screen completed the transformation. Pictured in Liverpool in 1993.

GM Buses 1697 was a former LUT Standard Fleetline that was converted by GMT into a single-decker after a low-bridge accident, initially to work a local Bury garage route around Holcombe that was too restricted for 10-metre Leyland Nationals. However, on this occasion in June 1990, it was awaiting departure from Piccadilly bus station in central Manchester.

This Daimler Fleetline was new to Southdown in 1970. By August 1991, when photographed in Llandudno, it was an open-topper with Crosville Wales as their HDG911, in use on the Happy Dragon service.

A cold day in January 1991 in Barnsley, and a picture of a Leyland Fleetline operated by South Yorkshire of Pontefract, purchased new by them in 1978.

Derby purchased examples of NCME-bodied Fleetlines in both low- and normal-height configurations during the seventies. Number 50, new in 1978, is an example of the former, pictured in the city centre in August 1991.

Nottinghamshire independent South Notts of Gotham purchased this Leyland-engined Daimler Fleetline in 1975. It has a NCME body style that had been popular with some of the BET fleets and which had its origins from the decade before. A visit to Nottingham in 1992 saw it still in service, but with the company now owned by Nottingham City Transport.

A former West Yorkshire PTE Leyland Fleetline in the Yorkshire Rider fleet. The bus is pictured on Piccadilly, in central Manchester, in September 1991, setting off on the long trans-Pennine trek back to Halifax.

In 1992, a venerable addition to the fleet of Pennine Blue of Dukinfield was this Leyland-engined Daimler Fleetline CRL6, which had been new as a double-doored bus to Southend Corporation in 1971. It came to Pennine Blue from South Notts of Gotham. Ashton bus station is the location in March 1993.

The distinctive livery of Leon of Finningley is evident in this shot, as is the equally distinctive Scottish Bus Group-style of destination screen on this former Western SMT Leyland Fleetline, new to them in 1978. The occasion is the annual gathering at the Sandtoft Trolleybus Museum in July 1993.

Bullock of Cheadle's AFA 489S was one of two Leyland Fleetlines in the fleet that had been new to Potteries independent Turner of Brown Edge, in this case back in 1978. This view from August 1993 sees it on Princess Street in central Manchester, meeting with the Metrolink tram tracks at Mosley Street.

A sunny day in Stranraer in 1993 sees Western Scottish SR869, a 1979 Fleetline built to low-height specification, passing by the depot. The attractive black, white, red and grey livery of the deregulated era is carried.

A Leyland Fleetline/NCME in the Yorkshire Rider fleet, photographed in Rochdale in October 1988. It was one of a batch of ten new to predecessor West Yorkshire PTE in 1976, which had originally been ordered by Halifax Corporation. The styling was an interesting mixture of the contemporary Standard and design elements from earlier vehicles.

A bright February day in Llandudno in 1997, with this Hughes Brothers (Alpine) Leyland Fleetline pictured near the company's yard. The bus had been new to Chester almost exactly twenty years previously and demonstrates their preferred low-height layout, together with side engine shrouds.

Cleveland Transit's last Leyland Fleetlines were the newest in terms of date registered, being the only examples to receive Y suffix marks, although in fact newer chassis had already been bodied for other operators. Here 151, registered in August 1982, is captured later in life in Middlesbrough in 1995.

A beautiful summer's day in Scarborough in July 1997, and Appleby of Louth was using this former Southend 33-foot Daimler Fleetline from 1975, by then converted to open-top. Note the Lancashire 'TD' registration, as Northern Counties registered Southend's vehicles locally at the time so that Southend could secure matching fleet and registration numbers.

Cleveland Transit approached Northern Counties to rebody one of their Leyland Leopards that had previously carried a Willowbrook dual-purpose body. The new body was constructed on a frame derived from a regular double-decker. The Leopard was delivered back to Cleveland Transit partially finished in 1986, with the operator completing the interior fittings. It is pictured in St Helens in 1993, by then owned by local independent South Lancs and nicknamed 'The Coffin'.

In addition to the bespoke rebody of the Leyland Leopard for Cleveland Transit, Northern Counties also rebodied twelve 1970 Leyland Atlanteans for them (replacing previous NCME bodies) between 1983 and 1986. Unusually, Fleetline, rather than Atlantean, engine cowls were fitted. By August 1995 SDC 146H had passed to Wirral operator Avon of Prenton and is pictured looking absolutely immaculate on rail replacement work in Liverpool.

Nottingham had specified a highly individual body style for its double-deck fleet from the 1960s into the first years of the deregulation era, evolving gradually over time. Northern Counties had been one of several suppliers, building mainly on Atlantean and Fleetline chassis. Nottingham's 432 demonstrates the final years of the Atlantean, featuring curved glass front windows, dual doors with single-panel front door, a raked destination screen, the use of smaller, imperial-measured five-bay window construction and a prominent High Energy Level Polymer (HELP) bumper.

A long-lived Leyland Atlantean in the Fylde fleet, the last survivor of a trio delivered to predecessor Lytham St Annes Corporation in 1970. By the time of this photo, near Blackpool's North Pier in August 1996, Fylde had been purchased by its larger neighbour and was being run as a separate unit, with vehicles painted in this blue variant of Blackpool livery.

Looking resplendent in the company's Bishop Auckland garage yard in April 1995 is this 33-foot Leyland Atlantean with OK, new to them in 1973.

A long-wheelbase Leyland Atlantean in the fleet of famous Lincolnshire independent Delaine of Bourne, pictured in Peterborough bus station in August 1996. This had been new to Whippet of Hilton in February 1973 and was acquired by Delaine in 1984. They already owned nearly identical ACT 540L, new to them the month after the Whippet example, and with consecutive chassis and body numbers.

Woeful weather in a soggy St Annes. Fylde Atlantean 70, bound for Blackpool, picks up grateful passengers on the seafront 1 service in September 1994. The driver will doubtless have his work cut out trying to cope with a defective wiper arm. The bus had been new to AA co-operative group member Young of Ayr in 1978.

Barrow Corporation purchased four Leyland Atlanteans to GM Standard specification between 1983 and 1984. Upon Barrow's collapse in 1989, all four passed to Stagecoach's Ribble fleet. By October 1996, after several further changes of ownership, this particular example was owned by Traction Group subsidiary, Lincoln, and is pictured leaving the city's bus station.

Over the years Fylde Transport was a regular customer for both new and second-hand Leyland Atlanteans that were mostly bodied by Northern Counties. In the nineties some of these were refurbished with Palatine front ends and the application of 'ageless' Northern Irish registrations. What had been EBV 88S was photographed in Lytham in September 1995, by which time Fylde was owned by neighbouring Blackpool Transport.

Captured in the Morecambe sunshine in June 1993 is Lancaster 187, one of a pair of former Southdown 'Queen Mary' class Leyland Titan PD3s, new as convertible open-toppers purchased in 1988. The former registration, 415 DCD, had been transferred onto a Leyland Leopard coach prior to the PD3's sale.

GMT took delivery of the fifth Leyland Olympian prototype (chassis number B45.05) in 1980. This shot in Ashton, in December 1992, sees it under GM Buses' ownership, on local service work with their Charterplan coaching unit, working out of the former North Western garage at Charles Street in Stockport.

From 1983 through to 1989 Northern Counties bodied 305 production Leyland Olympians purchased by Greater Manchester Transport and their successor GM Buses. Typical of these was 3044, new to GMT in 1984. Noteworthy is the gap between the first and second upstairs windows to accommodate the standard window arrangement on a chassis that was longer than the equivalent Standard-class Fleetline or Atlantean. The location is Liverpool in 1993 and 3044 is with GM Buses, competing against Merseybus on local services.

This ex-Nottingham Leyland Olympian was photographed on shuttle duties with Buffalo of Flitwick at Showbus, Woburn Abbey, in September 1991. This was one of a pair new in 1984 and built to Nottingham's typically idiosyncratic specification.

GMT purchased four Dennis Dominators with suitably adapted Standard bodywork, taking two pairs in 1980 and 1981. All four were disposed of at deregulation and all ended up with Buffalo of Flitwick. Former GMT 1437 is pictured, also on shuttle duties at Showbus, in September 1991.

South Yorkshire PTE purchased Dennis Dominators in the 1980s. Most of these had Alexander R-type bodies, but ten were bodied by Northern Counties in 1983. SYPTE specified many R-type features to aid standardisation of parts, giving the vehicles a unique appearance. All passed to South Yorkshire Transport at deregulation. 2315 was captured in Sheffield in their Mainline livery in June 1990.

Chester, having been a loyal Daimler and Leyland Fleetline customer in the seventies, turned initially to the Dennis Dominator when that model was no longer available. Number 104 was new in 1982 and is pictured on Foregate Street in the city centre in May 1994.

Essex-based Stephensons of Easingwold was the operator of this Dennis Dominator when photographed on London Underground rail replacement work at Euston station in October 1995. It had been new to Thamesdown as their number 56 in 1983.

Following the end of Fleetline production, Cleveland Transit also turned to the Dennis Dominator. Fourteen, all bodied by Northern Counties, entered the fleet between 1983 and 1986. Number 208 is pictured in Middlesbrough in August 1995.

A notable vehicle in the Capital Citybus fleet was this Dennis Dominator, which was one of three taken for evaluation in 1984 by London Transport and used on comparison trials on the 170 service alongside Leyland Olympians, Mark-II MCW Metrobuses and Volvo Ailsas. Number 203, by this time converted to single-door layout, is seen at rest at Euston in October 1995.

Following the initial four Dennis Dominators bought for evaluation, GMT took a further thirty NCME-bodied examples in 1985. Number 2008, by this point owned by GM Buses South, was photographed in Cateaton Street in Manchester – now much changed – in June 1994.

GMPTE was instrumental in getting Dennis to design the Domino midibus, derived from the larger Dominator. Twenty were delivered between late 1985 and early 1986, all bodied by Northern Counties to a bespoke design, and primarily to replace the existing Seddon Pennine 4 midis on the Centreline service linking Manchester's Piccadilly and Victoria stations. Here 1762, by this time a GM Buses vehicle, takes on passengers at Piccadilly station in March 1993.

Smith of Marple, near Stockport, was the owner of this former Cleveland Transit Bristol VRT when photographed outside the company's garage in July 1995. This was one of a batch new in 1977 and demonstrates the standard Transit bodywork specification of the time.

Nineteen distinctive 33-foot dual-doored low-height Bristol VRTs were delivered to Reading Transport between 1976 and 1977. This example eventually passed to Morley of Whittlesey and is pictured in Peterborough bus station in August 1997.

Two Scania BR112DH/NCMEs were purchased by GMT in 1983 and initially based at Leigh garage, before transfer to Atherton upon Leigh's closure. Under GM Buses' ownership the pair were transferred to Hyde Road in 1991 to be with the new Scania N113 buses allocated there. 1461 is pictured in Manchester, Piccadilly, in May of that year, still displaying its Atherton garage logo.

Derby purchased six Volvo Ailsa B55s with bodywork by Northern Counties in 1982. 119 was photographed in the city centre in August 1991. The windscreen notice, advertising 1p return fares, is evidence of the cut-throat competition going on at the time.

GMT purchased three Volvo Ailsas between 1980 and 1982. They were eventually disposed of after deregulation and were acquired by Lancaster. Here all three are captured in June sunshine at Lancaster's depot in Morecambe in 1993, a couple of months before Lancaster was taken over by Stagecoach.

This is former Tayside OSN 852Y, a 1983 Volvo Ailsa, languishing rather sadly near the yard of Wigan operator Finch of Higher Ince in December 2012. It still wears the livery of previous owner McDade of Hamilton, but the bus's service days were over. It went for scrap two years later.

GMT purchased three Volvo B10M double-deckers for evaluation in 1985. Last of the trio, 1483, was photographed with GM Buses North, still in GM Buses condition, in Wigan in January 1995.

Hartlepool 28 makes for a highly unusual recipient of Stagecoach corporate livery in this August 1995 view, following the group's takeover of this former municipal operator. This was one of six Dennis Falcon H/Northern Counties new, in 1985, to a body style that had barely changed since the 1960s.

Very similar to the Hartlepool example is this other Dennis Falcon – one of seven new to Ipswich in 1986. Eleven years later and former Ipswich 110 carries the gaudy livery of Choice Travel in this view in Wolverhampton bus station in August 1997.

The Dennis Falcon V double-decker was a rare beast indeed, with only six examples built. GMT took three with Northern Counties' bodies for evaluation in 1984, and then perhaps rued the day they did, because they weren't the most reliable of buses. The first of the trio, 1471, is seen on Mosley Street, Manchester, in March 1994, operating for GM Buses South, after having spent several years unused with GM Buses.

This Leyland Panther, one of a batch of ten new to Chesterfield in 1969, was still an active member of their fleet at the time of this visit to Sandtoft in July 1993. A repaint into former Chesterfield Corporation green and cream followed shortly afterwards and, upon withdrawal, the bus passed into preservation.

This 1970 ex-Southdown Daimler Fleetline was in use with Cheshire Constabulary as a mobile road safety exhibition unit in this view in Warrington town centre in March 1991.

Independent operator Lancashire United Transport purchased twenty lightweight Bristol LHs with NCME bodywork between late 1969 and early 1970. What had been LUT 320 was captured in March 1991, long after withdrawal from regular service work, in use as a mobile home.

A rear-end view in Ashton in 1993 of *Tilly Tameside*, a former Southdown 'Queen Mary' class Leyland PD3, owned by Tameside Council as a playbus. The upstairs conversion to accommodate a children's slide is noteworthy. *Tilly* had had a long life journey, moving all the way from southern England to an operator in the Isle of Skye, before a further move back south to her eventual role.

This Daimler Fleetline with double-door bodywork had been new to National Bus Company subsidiary City of Oxford in 1971. Depicted here, much later in life, it is in use as a non-PSV exhibition unit in Liverpool in 1993.

One of the more bizarre uses of an ex-GM Standard was by Westhoughton-based conservatory manufacturer Mark Forrest & Co., who added no end of double-glazed features to this Daimler Fleetline to publicise the business. Note that there is even internal foliage in place in this shot in Bolton in 1994.

Blackpool Operational Services Department owned this former Chesterfield 1971 Leyland Atlantean/Northern Counties, a double-doored vehicle built very much in the style of the emerging SELNEC Standard. It was one of a long line of non-PSV vehicles employed as workers' transport for tramway maintenance in the resort. September 1995 is the date.

The former GM Leyland Olympians had long careers, lasting well into the ownership of both First and Stagecoach. What had been GM numbers 3260 and 3236 are captured in December 2007, enjoying semi-retirement in the Stagecoach Manchester training fleet. The location is the yard adjacent to Stockport garage, with the iconic railway viaduct in the background.

This interesting vehicle started life in 1984 as A103 FPL, an 11-metre-long Leyland Olympian with ECW's express coach body of the time. Then, following major fire damage with subsequent owner Northumbria, it was rebodied in 1992 by Northern Counties. It is pictured here, owned by a Christian youth group, branded as Eden Bus, near Manchester Cathedral in May 2008.

A 2003 view outside the Manchester Museum of Transport of SELNEC EX1, the first Standard prototype, preserved lovingly to its former glory by the SELNEC Preservation Society. This and the other five in the batch were on Leyland Atlantean chassis ordered by Ashton Corporation prior to the SELNEC takeover.

A famous NCME-bodied bus, happily preserved in Manchester's Museum of Transport, is SHMD Joint Board's number 70; the unique double-deck Atkinson PD746, new in 1954, and made even more unusual by SHMD specifying a centre-entrance. Pictured passing Manchester's Victoria station in March 1996.

A posed study of a fine-looking municipal vehicle. Preserved Wigan Corporation 115, a 1958 Leyland Titan PD2, is pictured near the Museum of Transport on Boyle Street in Cheetham in May 1996. Wigan's characteristic marker lights either side of the destination screen, to help identify a corporation bus at night, can clearly be seen.

Northern Counties entered into an ultimately unsuccessful venture in the 1970s with Cheshire truck manufacturer Foden, the Foden-NC. Only seven chassis were ever produced, of which six – including a part-completed vehicle – were bodied by Northern Counties. Amazingly, two now survive in preservation, namely former West Midlands PTE 6300 and West Yorkshire PTE 7250, captured together at a rally organised by the North West Vehicle Restoration Trust at their base in Kirkby in 2018.

A 1982 Volvo Ailsa, privately preserved back to its original status as Cardiff 415, photographed entering the rally site at the 2018 Trans Lancs event in Heaton Park, Manchester. Cardiff had a fondness for the Ailsa, taking a total of thirty-six between 1982 and 1984, all bodied by NCME. For a while, as a result, they had the distinction of having the largest fleet of front-engined double-deckers for a council-owned company.

Preserved SELNEC Standard Daimler Fleetline 7206, an exhibit from the SELNEC Preservation Society's collection, gleams in the late evening light on Piccadilly in Manchester in June 2014. The occasion was the end of an evening tour organised for members of the PSV Circle. The offside window and staircase arrangement reveals it to be one of the forty-eight double-doored production examples.

Some may use the word 'atmospheric', but the cold truth is that Greengate, encapsulated by the railway line above, was a dank, dark and thoroughly miserable location, just on the Salford side of the Irwell. It was here that, from corporation days to the PTE era, the 'visiting' operators, such as Leigh Corporation and the independent Lancashire United Transport, had their city centre terminus. Preserved LUT 21, a 1959 Guy Arab IV, evokes those bygone days at the end of an enthusiasts' tour in January 1996. Subsequent urban redevelopment has seen the railway arches partly removed, and most of Greengate now basks at last in regular daylight.

Finally, a chance encounter with another former LUT Guy Arab on a visit to Uppermill, just as this book was being completed in May 2019. It is now in the private hire fleet of the Yorkshire Heritage Bus Company and is beautifully turned out in their black and white livery. Both bus and crew await the return of a wedding party, evident by the white ribbons and garland. The bus, an Arab V, had been new to LUT in 1963 and was their last open-platform half-cab decker, subsequent Arabs being of forward-entrance layout.